WE LIVE THE SONGS

a haiku collection

steve zmijewski

First edition

ISBN: 978-1-7371509-9-2

published by Laughing Ronin Press 2022

The action and intimate response of listening to music, the seeking and discovering and collecting, from a young age, has had a direct effect on me and my work, art, whatever you would like to call it... this existence of mine.

The bands and musicians that I love and their songs serve as the backbeat and vital bedding to my creativity, more than any writer or painter has.

In a way, this is an expression of gratitude.

Though not nearly complete, from my own point of view, at least, but I'd say I cover a lot of ground here.

The following pages feature plenty of essential and all-time favorites. Largely foundational stuff and so many moments and mileposts spent drenched in the sounds.

Whether you know the band, song or album or immediately recognize a reference, or not, I hope you can pull some meaning from these poems.
Thanks for reading.

We live the songs.

And we must see that they outlive every last one of us.

WE LIVE THE SONGS

Uncorked red wine flows
Six nights of recollecting
The bugs overgrown

went walking with the cassette single and its cardboard sleeve

Grade seven I thought
River of Dreams was neck deep-
Hope floats still in reach

adding to the made up moving picture in my head
every sunday car ride when he played his tapes

I can't dance, won't sing
Father child make do and bend
Rain drops keep falling

take your time don't walk too fast you awkward simple man

Did I know it then
Lawn seat, age twelve, first of tons
Skynyrd set the stage

vs the monstars in the rearviewmirror

At shits and showers
Took them in with me to wash
Years to find my place

it's dangerous to go alone into the superunknown

Hot pine needle tea.
Praying for a black hole sun.
Take this. Seize the day.

gotta look sharp on your radio

Before I knew cool
Mixtapes of Costello hits
I wanted to be

wide eyed and wasting time but the playlists are worth it

Blue black white and pink
These were important to me
And my painting sprees

as we all fall I cannot help but hate

You can play puppets
Let me propel the lightning
Give justice to all

heavy metal mixes for pickup games

Cracks grow on home courts
Floodlights bare roots and trends kill
to see a new day

better go and beware (if her horns are in the air)

Ozzy grins on me
Sabbath shines in lack of light
This notes for Aunt Sue

never met a wise man

Convey thanks for the
eye opening, door busting
sense of angst and self

i wanted another, but as nearly all i write, it won't say enough

Throw me in the fire
On most days its makes most sense
I run back to you

try but you can't bring me down

Bully drank cologne
Wore a GB shirt to fool
every other day

beginning of the end seen in the light of hindsight beyond sight

Stayed asleep in class
Feet propped on book rack under
crush in the green coat

it's so predictable

Life aint so peachy
Locked keys in your running car
Dreaming about sex

laugh all you need, just admit, $3 bill is still great

Never for nookie
Just limping with the bizkit
Better than no one

rage, because anger is (an energy)

blood pressure raised red flags rose a fist in a fit
let tha guilty hang

i'd like to buy candy for a girl who doesn't know i exist

Felt trapped in a box
But my castle was empty
Make some space for me

the football was aimed for the boombox
then she moved her face and i was glad

Killing me softly
Rosy freckles lit the room
Don't touch that dial

**believed in science long before it was looked down on
and ignored**

Fell upon side stage
Discovered an obsession
that would redefine

10/26/99 cut school and went to the wiz

There's plenty to air
You told us to make ourself
I've been trying since

give me art and sustenance

Magic marker used
A trigger to ink some truth
Leave this sphere surprised

16

miss the days of gibbler rock NJ

Close, connected in
those moments. Sore throats off key,
that's what we adored.

more than 20 summers passed

Outside my window
missed opportunities to
join them in the van

fuck the movie, save your life, lose the girl

Midtown near all things
Watch this place burn to the ground
Ten seconds too late

remembering us coming back from a dive

Wake the dead in me
Joined voices break the silence
Beer splashed into shoes

woah woah woah...GO!

black dove jacket patch
wearing that was a big deal
meant for youth anthems

this is the part (or it's supposed to be)

The system is broke
Says a man long overboard
Forging new end plans

hey jonah, won't you, if it's too far, take an aeroplane

Last aisle yelling
rock my house once more, please just
be quiet and drive

and tonight i feel like a bore

Lying in the grass
White pony, her diamond eyes
May never let go

and happiness wasn't a thief we could catch

Will of superman
mislead by lady of peace.
She lives in my frown.

oh, fuck it, look alive

Nada surf through space
Underrated in the sea
Cool waves push on by

                    stand by me the same today as yesterday

Black spot on the sun
Feel the pain of everyone
I am not afraid

                              surprising event or thing

Error of our ways
Famous last words on repeat
Ya gotta believe

love you similar to how a fellow mets fan may cherish '86

Kevin—Kev, you make
blood boil, clocks move and ghosts rest.
I wish we were friends.

Oh, I am sorry.
That last did not perform well-
Like gum you have stuck.

No,no.. not again.
These truth poems of struggled terms
fail to tell it clear.

cup of coffee when i can

Are we built to spill
Leaking mornings like our cars
My guts hold their ground

what is life if not for you

Imagine   embraced in bed
for twenty-five hours.
Once, I thought we would.

the first star i see may be a car (wreck)

cold, collapse, change course
was clarity found unbound
fluttering its wings

　　　　　　leaves turn to brown old friends conversing
　　　　　　weeping laughing through the box

Fifty-eight Stone Street
Simon and Garfunkel crooned
Worlds spun around us

　　　　　　　　　　　　looks like rain again

Little league at heart
Fair weather soaked on brick walls
The last thing she said

this is not a fugazi tshirt

Flex your idle heads
Think about the importance
Ethics and contempt

always legwork but that's no reason to stop

Gotten old, distant
I'll hardly forget the fests
Bleeding hearts booming

i've often said i wanted to write this play

to tell the story-
An ugly organ cast with
lost green appleseeds

it's funny how first i forgot your name

Oneself at Birch Hill
A sad assemblage of stars
Slow danced in Roseland

skipped details for makeshift boxing gloves

Faint laughs graze silence
Her knapsack filled to the brim
Jealous sounds anxious

best friend hard to handle now

Free drinks, full of fear
We gotta catch that last train
Got blues high and low

honorary titles of affection drifting away overhead

Nodding at her side
We had our own subway car
My bones on display

but i won't tell anyone (i guess, except for you)

Back to hating friends
They do not know who they are
Acts of conspiring

take me out or pull me under

Bottled up, clung to
transatlanticism and
trouble will find me

every time i hear the crackle and that B.B. sample

Hell yeah! Standing outside a
broken phone booth with
money in my hand!

silver bullet and a contingency plan

Dreamin' up night moves.
Meet me in Machu Picchu
when your soul's heavy.

turn it on that distaste for lack of effort

and away it rolled
kick push kick never better
how absurd pain is

wanderers well wishers pointless forever

Some nights I can't pre-
tend to understand. Won't you
help me survive them.

jaws 3, bash bros 0

Goddamn, we're too fucking good!
Let's get the fuck fuck
fuck fuck out of here!

somedays you'd think the world was ending

Regina, it's me
I don't know what should be done
Anything at all

maybe you were just a mirage

Circle that love song
What feels wrong is mostly right
Hi-fi in your eyes

the relief next to me, you are all i need

We thought it would be the songs of summer
that melted up our dashboard

11-6-16

Such great heights you are
bound. Breathe in for all to see.
Move mountains, my boy.

2-20-19

The moon is full, it salutes.
And with you snow stuck
closer to our heart.

7-30-20

Latches are shifting
Our love is everlasting
Look back and endure

stop talking stop talking will you stop

talking making sense
I'm taking back my felt words
And walking backward

keep it down the kids are asleep dreaming

Music in our hips
Swaying beneath setting sons
Cause they pulled us up

the secret life of disappearing

Whispering the words
stay alive in my pillow.
Dawn arrives too quick

displeasure exemplified, song chills the spine

Hiding in the lines,
piano became the tooth
biting this state of...

the kids like it (yeah, yeah, yeah)

Bad Operation,
from New Orleans, praise you for
reconnecting me

Without all the noise
What does a life amount to
Spare me your reply

Heavy is my head
Escaping weight of planets
You see   I lived these

As salt pinched to wounds
As state of mind spoken up
As plastic worn through

When
all we sincerely want is to
sing some fucking words,
honest and
wholeheartedly.

https://open.spotify.com/playlist/4aWfo9JheTnI2cjvky
XEMZ?si=1c93242ef9b64bb2

Steve Zmjewski is a dad of three staggering little boys and at this leg of his life, that is what he leads with. They are his inspiration, the reason he has a chest full of breath.

Eatontown, New Jersey is where he and the family currently reside.

Steve has been writing his sensitivity out, as a way to cope and make sense of all the stuff in and around him, for quite some time now. Most recent, he saw the release of Hobo Scarecrow Connecting Hollow Dots (Between Shadows Press); and Cored, Commuting Love, Sored (Maverick Duck Press). Several of his poems have been included in anthologies published by A.B. Baird Publishing and Neon Sunrise Publishing.

He and his wife, Lindsey, run Two Key Customs and have put out The Covid Collab; Hope, Sticks & Hollow Bones; and Shit from an Old Notebook, among others, with much more to come.

Find him at instagram.com/catchstevez
Site, Shop and more found at linktr.ee/Catchstevez

Made in the USA
Middletown, DE
03 February 2022

60168484R00022